THE RESILIENCE POCKETBOOK

Janine Waldman & Paul Z Jackson
Drawings by Phil Hailstone

"Sometimes life makes me feel like I am spinning plates in a circus, in danger of them all crashing down! A strong sense of personal resilience allows me to manage these challenges and bounce back from any 'crashes'. This book has given me both fantastic insight and practical guidance, allowing me to examine and further develop my own resilience. Highly recommended!"
Gemma Todd, Head of Human Resources, Imperial London Hotels

"A great quick-reference practical guide incorporating a useful mix of interesting new ideas and tried and tested favourites."
Helen Rowe, Head of Brand & Communications Research, Kantar TNS

"As an ex-serviceman and current business owner, the advice in this book will keep me moving forward on my toughest days."
Ryan Green, Managing Director, Pebble

Published by:
Management Pocketbooks Ltd
Laurel House, Station Approach, Alresford, Hants SO24 9JH, U.K.
Tel: +44 (0)1962 735573 Fax: +44 (0)1962 733637
Email: sales@pocketbook.co.uk
Website: www.pocketbook.co.uk

All rights reserved. No part of this publication may be reproduced, stored in a retrieval system or transmitted in any form, or by any means, electronic, mechanical, photocopying, recording or otherwise, without the prior permission of the publishers.

© Janine Waldman & Paul Z Jackson 2017

This edition published 2017

ISBN 978 1 906610 92 0
E-book ISBN 978 1 908284 52 5

British Library Cataloguing-in-Publication Data – A catalogue record for this book is available from the British Library.

Design, typesetting and graphics by **efex ltd**.   Printed in U.K.

CONTENTS

INTRODUCTION 5
The importance of resilience, definitions, resilience for organisations, now more than ever, the case of Kerry, two key tasks, do's and don'ts

RESILIENCE AT WORK 23
Bouncebackability, the business case, the costs & benefits, what drains resilience at work?, make it work

YOU AND YOUR RESILIENCE 29
Born or made?, where do you get it from?, how resilient are you today?, resilient recall, focus on what you can influence, be proactive, do something new, stress vs pressure

FOUR DIMENSIONS OF RESILIENCE 43
Physical, energy guzzlers & sources, activity; Mental, activity; Emotional, activity; Social, communities of support, activity; which route to take?, who you gonna call?

RESILIENCE TOOLKIT 59
Solutions-focused tools, the nature of tools, your toolkit, building a platform, future perfect, scale, counters, affirm, small actions, what else?, what's better?

MISTAKES & PROGRESS, FAILURE & RECOVERY 81
Join the anti-perfectionist league, are you perfect?, on a scale of 1 to 10, the traps of perfectionism, mind your language, recovering from failure, after a crisis ask what worked, fight, flight, freeze or flow, how to use and apply the flow model, solutions not problems, the progress principle

TEAMS: SPREADING RESILIENCE 99
The impact, flourishing in adversity, improving the atmosphere, what's going well – team meetings, tell empowering stories, display success, find out what's wanted, more sociability at work, finding fault or future focus?, quotes & action

ACKNOWLEDGMENTS

We wish to thank all our friends, colleagues and clients who have contributed to this book. In no particular order, that includes Anton Stellamans, Liselotte Baeijaert, Martin Coburn, and the dozens of participants in our resilience programmes and workshops.

We'd also like to thank those writers who have gone before us and whose work we have drawn upon. They have articulated the important concepts of resilience, done the hard research and provided a foundation without which this would not have been possible.

> *'A good half of the art of living is resilience.'*
> **Alain de Botton**

Introduction

INTRODUCTION

THE IMPORTANCE OF RESILIENCE

Resilience is the ability to face the constant change and struggles of the day and still come out working well. Resilience means bouncing back from difficulties or being equipped so that you don't go down in the first place. It matters because it is all about your readiness to meet the world in a resourceful state.

With resilience, however tough things get, you can regroup and manage whatever you have to deal with and keep going, especially necessary in these turbulent economic times.

When you are resilient, you manage uncertainty well and continue to make progress. On the other hand, if you are not resilient, you risk burning yourself out through stress, sickness and conflict.

INTRODUCTION

HOW THIS BOOK WILL HELP YOU

This book is about how you can build your personal resilience.

It's crammed full of tips, tools and techniques we've collected over the years. You can use these to help you bounce back from difficulties, and to make yourself more equipped to face the daily challenges of work and life.

Let's face it, everyone has difficulties in their lives and we're keen to share the range of techniques we have discovered that help us through many tricky moments, occasional crises and the worst rough patches.

By reading this book, you'll find ways to uncover and develop your own resources and those of your teams.

INTRODUCTION

HOW THIS BOOK WILL HELP YOU

You will find out how to:

- Recover faster when things go wrong – even when it's not easy, you'll be better equipped to overcome difficulties and make progress
- Reveal and make smarter use of your existing resources, skills and attributes. Yes, your ingredients for resilience are already largely in place
- Promote feelings of success in those around you as a leader, manager or colleague
- Tackle such enemies of resilience as conflict, difficulty, and feelings of inadequacy and failure
- Gain confidence in your innate ability to adapt and respond

As you read the book and do the exercises, notice which ideas resonate most with you. Then, next time you are faced with a particularly tough challenge, pick the book up again, remind yourself of the relevant techniques and start to apply them.

INTRODUCTION

ABOUT US

We are well placed to write this Pocketbook, having run many successful workshops around the world on the topic.

We approach resilience from a distinctive, solutions-focused perspective.

What this means is that instead of focusing on the details of a problem, we concentrate on developing a 'solution' by identifying what's wanted by the parties involved and discovering what already works for them.

One of the central tenets of this approach is to make use of what's there, unearthing people's strengths and finding ways of applying those strengths to work situations.

By drawing out knowledge, resources, skills and ideas for action, we are encouraging a resilience-based strategy that enables people to take quick, confident steps towards improving their performance and making significant, lasting changes.

INTRODUCTION

WHY RESILIENCE MATTERS

We borrow the metaphor of resilience from nature and from the realm of material sciences. Why does it matter to us? It matters because it's fundamental to how we shape our identity.

We are social beings, shaped by all the events of our lives. We need to be able to make meaning out of what happens to us.

If you share a story with others about who you are, you are joining a public exchange that creates social coherence. Resilience is our collective power to create our own meaning.

INTRODUCTION

WHY RESILIENCE MATTERS

You need resilience in times of adversity. The need can be triggered by illness, job loss, financial problems, natural disasters, relationship break-ups or the death of loved ones.

Perhaps less dramatically, it can be prompted by the frustrations of not getting the job or the contract or the partner you want.

Instead of responding well, you may have unhealthy coping mechanisms such as drinking too much, over-eating or taking drugs. Or simply doing nothing.

Then there are times you may feel overwhelmed by the sheer weight of daily life.

Building your resilience enables you to cope better with the inevitable difficulties you face.

INTRODUCTION

DEFINITIONS OF RESILIENCE

So what exactly is resilience? Here are some descriptions that you may find helpful:

- Materials are termed resilient if, having been bent or stretched, they go back to their original shape

- Resilience is the capacity to rebuild and grow from adversity. Think of pruning a plant that re-grows more vigorously after a trim

- Resilience is bending rather than breaking under pressure, persevering and adapting when faced with challenges

- Resilience is whatever helps you navigate a stressful and complex world

INTRODUCTION

DEFINITIONS OF RESILIENCE

If you're looking for an official definition, here's the American Psychological Association:

'The process of adapting well in the face of adversity, trauma, tragedy, threats and even significant sources of stress, such as family and relationship problems, serious health problems, or workplace and financial stresses.'

And this is British Standard 65000:

'BS 65000 defines organisational resilience as the ability to anticipate, prepare for, respond and adapt to events – both sudden shocks and gradual change. That means being adaptable, competitive, agile and robust.'

That's right, organisations can be resilient too, just like individual people, and – as you'll see – teams.

INTRODUCTION

RESILIENCE FOR ORGANISATIONS

This book is primarily about your personal resilience, but it's worth noting that resilience is increasingly on the agenda of organisations. Companies want to know, for example, how best to survive when talented and knowledgeable people leave, and how to cope collectively with financial or market shocks.

On the international stage, the British government Department for International Development (DFID), recently committed £140 million through their Building Resilience and Adaptation to Climate Extremes and Disasters (BRACED) programme. Our resilience to climate change may determine the future of the world.

INTRODUCTION

NOW MORE THAN EVER

We live in a VUCA world of work that offers little certainty.

VUCA is a military-derived term, meaning Volatile, Uncertain, Complex and Ambiguous. An old adage says, *'Generals are always planning for the last war'*. The next invariably features an unexpected aspect that demands quicker responses, more adaptation and more resilience.

Times are tough, budgets are tight. You can no longer be certain that a job is for life.

INTRODUCTION

THE CASE OF KERRY: TRIALS & TRIATHLONS

CASE EXAMPLE

Kerry was new in her job as head of training for a large manufacturing company. She'd done well to get this appointment – a step up from her previous firm – yet things didn't seem to be working out. The projects she had tried to initiate had not taken off and she was having increasing difficulties with her team members.

After three months, her boss told her that her probationary period was being extended for a further three, and that if results didn't improve, her contract would be terminated.

Having been successful in previous jobs, Kerry was at an all-time low, feeling completely overwhelmed. She seriously considered handing in her notice.

That evening she went out for a drink with her good friend George. He asked her if she really wanted to quit. After thinking about it, Kerry realised that ultimately she wanted to do a good job and prove they had hired the right person.

Encouraged, George asked her what successes she'd had – however small – in the time she'd been at the factory. Kerry identified a few minor triumphs and recalled the times when her team had done as she asked.

INTRODUCTION

THE CASE OF KERRY: TRIALS & TRIATHLONS

CASE EXAMPLE

She also started to look at what she was good at. Being a triathlon runner, Kerry had stamina, discipline and the ability to set and achieve small goals in order to reach a much larger one.

She went home feeling a lot better. The next day, rather than discussing her failures further and berating her team for their poor behaviour, she smiled at everybody and started to approach her work as if it was a triathlon – with discipline, rigour, focus, small steps and long-term goals. Her change of attitude was a turning point. Three months later the job was hers.

INTRODUCTION

TWO KEY TASKS

1 Write down what resilience means to you and where it could be important in your life and work.

2 Take a moment to think about the times of difficulty or stress that you've experienced: how did you come through them? How resilient do you feel right now?

INTRODUCTION

DO'S AND DON'TS OF RESILIENCE

Here are some tips that we've crafted over the years to guide you on your journey towards building and maintaining your resilience:

DON'TS

- ✗ Don't focus on problems, deficits, blame and weaknesses.
- ✗ Don't dwell on your problems or wonder why you are not more resilient.
- ✗ Don't go over the details of your failings and mistakes.
- ✗ Don't operate in isolation or forget that you are part of an interactional world.

DO'S

- ✓ Do identify what you want and what result you are aiming for.
- ✓ Do focus instead on how resilient you would like to be.
- ✓ Do visualise yourself as successful, competent and resourceful.
- ✓ Do take note of who else can be involved in growing your resilience.

INTRODUCTION

DO'S AND DON'TS OF RESILIENCE

DON'TS

- ✗ Don't believe you can read people's minds or always guess their intentions.
- ✗ Don't get into negative thought spirals about your inadequacy and how it gets more and more difficult every time.
- ✗ Don't assume the worst is going to happen or that things will be as bad as before.
- ✗ Don't fret about what you haven't got, what's missing or where you lack skills or expertise in any given situation.
- ✗ Don't imagine the worst possible scenario that might unfold in the future.

DO'S

- ✓ Do stick to the facts and pay attention to what is actually happening.
- ✓ Do strengthen your positive thought cycles with evidence of how you have coped, learned and succeeded.
- ✓ Do respond and adapt in the moment to what you see and hear.
- ✓ Do identify what you do have, the resources (both inner and outer) that are already available to you.
- ✓ Do explore what a 'good' future would look like – how would you know things are as you would like them to be?

INTRODUCTION

DO'S AND DON'TS OF RESILIENCE

DON'TS

- ✗ Don't look on the past with a view to what failed and didn't work.
- ✗ Don't see the present as weighted against you, given all your weaknesses and lack of ability.
- ✗ Don't use complicated jargon about your personality type as an excuse, because 'code-red watery introverts aren't good at leading projects'.
- ✗ Don't assume that what worked in one situation will work in every situation.

DO'S

- ✓ Do look back and identify what you've learned, experienced or noticed that might be useful in the current situation.
- ✓ Do stay aware of the skills and attributes you can access when faced with a tough situation.
- ✓ Do use clear and simple language: 'Here's what I want to happen…'.
- ✓ Do treat every situation on its merits, seeking out relevant actions and resources that fit there.

The do's and don'ts may look simple enough, yet it can take time and effort to master these arts across the wide variety of situations you are going to face.

INTRODUCTION
INSPIRATION

> *'The greatest glory in living lies not in never falling, but in rising every time we fall.'*
> **Nelson Mandela**

> *'I've got 99 problems and 86 of them are completely made up scenarios in my head that I'm stressing about for absolutely no reason.'*
> **Source unknown**

Resilience at work

RESILIENCE AT WORK
BOUNCEBACKABILITY

Resilience is sometimes called 'bouncebackability', a term reputedly coined by Iain Dowie, then manager of football club Crystal Palace, who famously described his team as showing '... *great bouncebackability*' when they overturned a losing position.

How do you bounce back from difficulties and failure at work? And how do you reduce the bouncing, so that the lows are neither so low nor so frequent? You might start by battling with perfectionism and changing your attitude towards mistakes. Without a need to get things right all the time, you'll be more able to forgive yourself for trivial errors, and more prepared to join in with new, healthy activities that will enhance your resilience.

Of course, absolute accuracy is needed at times, as when writing a report or compiling figures, but not everything requires it. Conversations with colleagues, for example, or making a presentation do not require perfection – in fact, there may not even be such a thing – and they don't need to be judged the same way.

Perfectionism can leave you feeling constantly dissatisfied and self-critical – and less willing to give things a go, even if it would be to your advantage to do so.

RESILIENCE AT WORK

THE BUSINESS CASE

Let's look more closely at the business case for building resilience at work.

Stress is a significant cost to business, accounting for **37%** of all work-related ill health cases and **45%** of all working days lost to ill health in 2015/6*.

Resilience at work means recovering quickly from mistakes, dealing with difficult situations calmly and confidently, and rebounding after career disasters. A resilient attitude is thus the key to your progress at work. With more resilient people at work, the teams and the organisation itself become more resilient.

Resilient organisations are those that cope well with shocks and failures. For example, they build in spare capacity, so that if one part of the system fails, there is still back up. *Lean* is currently a popular idea, but too much stripping to the bone can be disastrous. People and their organisations need a certain amount of slack. It is much harder to be resilient when resources are stretched to the limit.

*Source: http://www.hse.gov.uk/statistics/causdis/stress/ quoting HSE 'Work related Stress, Anxiety and Depression Statistics in Great Britain 2016.'

RESILIENCE AT WORK

THE COSTS & BENEFITS

Let's explore in more detail what's at stake. What are the costs and benefits for you and for your organisation?

Unresilient	Resilient
People lack confidence/ burn out	People bounce back from difficulty and failure more quickly
Performance is poor	Potential is recognised and made use of
A lack of creativity leads to missed opportunities	Creativity and flexibility increase
Indecision and isolation	Teams work better together
High sickness/ turnover	Staff stay longer
Viral air of negativity	More attractive working environment
Poor employer image	Good reputation

RESILIENCE AT WORK

WHAT DRAINS RESILIENCE AT WORK?

What's the biggest drain on resilience at work? In a survey of 835 British employees 75% of respondents said it was managing difficult people or office politics (see table). This was closely followed by stress brought on by overwork and by having to withstand personal criticism.

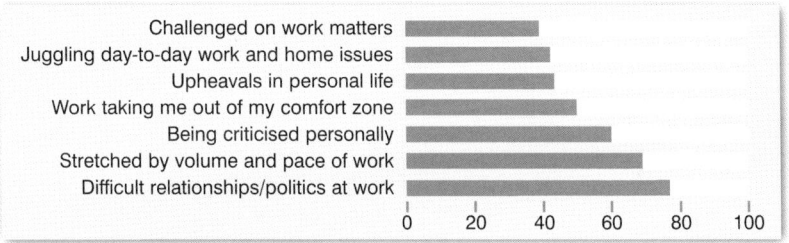

Adapted from *Tough at the Top?* by Sarah Bond & Gillian Shapiro

A separate study published by EU-OSHA (2009) suggests that 50% - 60% of all lost working days are due to stress.

RESILIENCE AT WORK

MAKE IT WORK

What drains **you** at work?
Which of these can you start to tackle?

> *'Your "I can" is more important than your IQ.'*
> **Robin Sharma**

> *'I don't measure a man's success on how high he climbs, but on how high he bounces when he hits rock bottom.'*
> **George S. Patton Junior**

You & your resilience

YOU & YOUR RESILIENCE

BORN OR MADE?

So, what about you and your resilience? It's tempting to think that resilience is a fixed personality trait, maybe even something that we are born with. But be reassured, it is something that can be learned and developed by anyone.

It's also easy to assume that those you view as most resilient are free from negative emotions and thoughts, remaining optimistic in all types of challenging situations. However, those who appear resilient have first been through a crucible of searing experiences, developing techniques to help them cope and allowing them to effectively navigate their way around or through crises.

You can see on the next page how resilience is viewed as hard-earned and personal.

YOU & YOUR RESILIENCE

WHERE DO YOU GET IT FROM?

The same 835 people (see page 27) were also asked where their resilience came from.

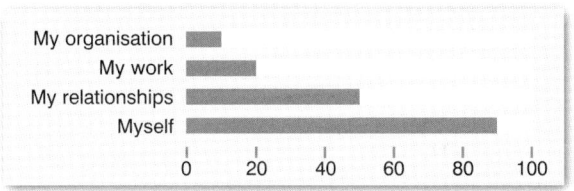

Adapted from *Tough at the Top?* by Sarah Bond & Gillian Shapiro

Fully 90% of the people questioned said, *'from myself'*; 50% said, *'from my relationships'*, and barely 10% said, *'from my organisation'*.

How resilient you are, how effectively you deal with difficulty and bounce back from failure is squarely in your own hands…. so, let's get to work.

YOU & YOUR RESILIENCE

HOW RESILIENT ARE YOU TODAY?

Before you start embedding the practices that will strengthen your resilience, you can give yourself a baseline measure of how resilient you feel right now.

For each statement, rate yourself from 1 = strongly disagree to 5 = strongly agree.

	1 2 3 4 5
1. I'm usually optimistic. I see difficulties as temporary and expect to overcome them.	☐☐☐☐☐
2. I tolerate high levels of ambiguity and uncertainty about situations.	☐☐☐☐☐
3. I adapt quickly to new developments.	☐☐☐☐☐
4. I'm good at bouncing back from difficulties.	☐☐☐☐☐
5. I'm playful. I find the humour in rough situations and can laugh at myself.	☐☐☐☐☐
6. I'm able to recover emotionally from losses and setbacks. Feelings of disappointment don't last long.	☐☐☐☐☐
7. I have friends to talk with. I can express my feelings to others and ask for help.	☐☐☐☐☐
8. I feel self-confident, appreciate myself and have a healthy concept of who I am.	☐☐☐☐☐
9. I'm curious. I ask questions. I want to know how things work. I like to try new things.	☐☐☐☐☐

YOU & YOUR RESILIENCE

HOW RESILIENT ARE YOU TODAY?

	1 2 3 4 5
10. I learn valuable lessons from my own and others' experiences.	☐☐☐☐☐
11. I'm good at solving problems. I mix logic, creativity and common sense.	☐☐☐☐☐
12. I'm good at making things work well. I'm often asked to lead groups and projects.	☐☐☐☐☐
13. I feel comfortable with my paradoxical complexity.	☐☐☐☐☐
14. I prefer to work without a written job description or close supervision. I'm more effective when I'm free to do what I think is best.	☐☐☐☐☐
15. I'm a good, empathic listener.	☐☐☐☐☐
16. I read people well and trust my intuition.	☐☐☐☐☐
17. I'm non-judgmental about others and adapt to people's different personality styles.	☐☐☐☐☐
18. I've been made stronger and better by difficult experiences.	☐☐☐☐☐
19. I've converted misfortune into good luck and found benefits in bad experiences.	☐☐☐☐☐
20. I'm very durable. I hold up well during tough times.	☐☐☐☐☐

Adapted from: Resiliency Quiz, Al Siebert, Resiliency Center

YOU & YOUR RESILIENCE

WHAT'S THE SCORE?

Scoring:

80 or higher	– outstandingly resilient, keep going
65-80	– more resilient than not
50-65	– fairly resilient and could be more so
40-50	– struggling
40 or under	– it's time to take urgent action

It's up to you

Everybody has the capacity to be resilient. Resilience has driven human growth for centuries, as our species has survived through many hardships. And you can increase your mental and physical toughness by your own practice and by deliberately reaching out to other people to create support for each other. It won't happen automatically – it's a question of choice.

The rest of this chapter shares strategies we've found that will help you build your personal resilience should you choose to do so.

YOU & YOUR RESILIENCE

RESILIENT RECALL

Drawing on your positive past experiences provides insights and clues as to how to deal with future events. Try out this three-step Resilient Recall process to uncover how you could put your personal history to good use in the future.

STEP 1: Think of a time when you felt particularly resilient – a time when you responded positively to something challenging. Take a moment to jot down:
- What you were doing
- Why it was that you felt resilient at that particular time
- What was going on for you that qualifies your response as resilient
- What other people would have noticed about you at that moment

STEP 2: Now make a list of all the skills, qualities and resources that made up your resilience on that occasion.

STEP 3: As you reflect on that time, and the skills, qualities and resources that enabled you to be so resilient, note how you might draw on these again when you are next in need of them.

YOU & YOUR RESILIENCE

FOCUS ON WHAT YOU CAN INFLUENCE

Do you waste energy worrying about matters you simply cannot influence? Consistently putting your energy into worrying about things beyond your control is a one-way ticket to anxiety, upset and stress.

Author and leadership guru Stephen Covey recommends focusing only on those concerns that you have control over. He outlines the 'circle of concern' as all of the stuff that worries you – and then a smaller 'circle of influence' (within the larger 'circle of concern') that contains only what you can realistically control.

His point is that you should spend your energy only on those variables that you can do something about. Focus only on problems that lie within your 'circle of influence'.

This turns out to be not as easy as it sounds, because the more passionate you feel about something the more you want to protect or fix it. Regardless of whether or not you have influence, if you care you want to tackle every problem as it emerges. So beware!

YOU & YOUR RESILIENCE

FOCUS ON WHAT YOU CAN INFLUENCE

Try shifting attention from those things you can't influence to those you can – rather than being reactive, be proactive as outlined below.

Covey's Circles of Influence and Concern

Reactive Focus	Change Your Focus	Proactive Focus
You focus your time and energy on your own problems and concerns. You blame others and you don't take responsibility.	You begin focusing on the things within your control and you start making a difference.	You devote your time and energy to changing what is in control. Your life improves and you stop blaming others.

YOU & YOUR RESILIENCE

FOCUS ON WHAT YOU CAN INFLUENCE

Here are some tips to help you increase your proactivity.

1. Next time an issue arises, ask yourself, *'How likely is it that this issue can be resolved or progressed by my actions?'* If the answer is less than 10% - cut your losses and move on.

2. Ask yourself, *'Is this even worth my influence?'* You have limited energy, so spend it on what most matters to you. Challenge your judgments on whether or not these concerns are really worthy of your time.

3. Use others to help you gain perspective. Sometimes you'll be unsure of whether or not an item is under your control. If you're too immersed in a problem, it's tricky to be objective. Get some perspective from those around you: present the facts and ask a trusted colleague for their opinion.

YOU & YOUR RESILIENCE

BE PROACTIVE

As you progress at work you will face competition, conflict, rejection and criticism on the road to advancement, acceptance and praise.

One way you can seem to avoid the worst of the negatives is by procrastinating or simply not putting yourself forward. You refuse to play the game. But this comes with clear downsides, such as limiting your learning and your progress. A more fruitful option is to take on the challenge and commit to dealing with the trials along the way. That is both exciting and scary, and it brings your resilience into the equation.

Logically, neither rejection nor criticism can hurt you, but it is usually easier to turn back than to face their pitiless gaze. Hold your nerve and you find that the fear is the price of progress. Expect fear and welcome it. Don't panic. Its message is simply that you should be alert and equipped to face the challenge.

If criticism hurts, it means you care. Get higher quality criticism and use it to learn and to improve. Many of us tend to be our own harshest critics, so replace your negative voice with the constructive criticism of people you trust who are willing to help you.

YOU & YOUR RESILIENCE

DO SOMETHING NEW

Being proactive also involves doing something new or different – for example taking on a new project at work, starting a hobby or learning a language.

A benefit of being more open to taking on new opportunitles is that you can use them to practise and increase your resilience. In that mode, you see setbacks as transient. When you are an active agent, you reap the benefits of taking control of both the situation and your emotional responses. Change and conflict now seem natural, all part of the process.

YOU & YOUR RESILIENCE

STRESS VS PRESSURE

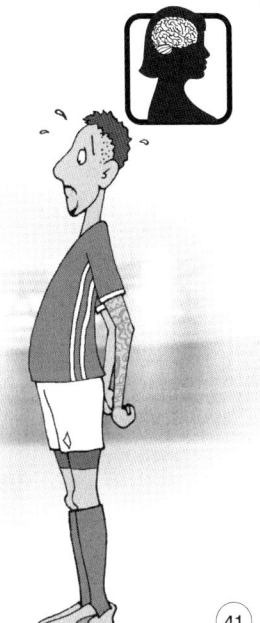

As you work on your resilience, you may find it helps to make a distinction between everyday stress and high-stakes pressure.

There's a direct connection between resilience and other qualities that we recognise as positive and desirable in people. Courage, for example, is displayed when people feel strong. And that strength is the same as the feeling of resilience to the pressures that surround you.

The question then is how to deal with pressure. And it's worth making a distinction between stress – the stuff of everyday life that you must constantly deal with, and pressure – the special, peak moments when you are on the pitch and the crowd is watching as you take the penalty.

YOU & YOUR RESILIENCE

STRESS VS PRESSURE

You feel the **stress** only at the times when you lack the immediate resources to handle and deal with the contingencies of everyday life. **Pressure** is when the consequences are ramped up and there is (apparently) more at stake, with more people caring about the outcomes.

You may want to take extra measures to equip yourself for pressure, such as training, coaching, practising with simulations. The key to dealing with everyday stress is your collection of coping tactics. These may be different from your special strategies for managing pressure.

The connection between them is that you should maintain yourself in good condition against the everyday stresses, so that you have plenty in reserve for those heightened, high-stake moments of pressure.

> *'Ultimately… there are no problems. Only situations – to be dealt with now, or to be left alone and accepted as part of the present moment until they change or can be dealt with.'*
> **Eckhart Tolle, The Power of Now**

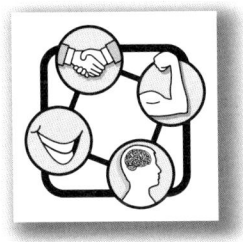

Four dimensions of resilience

FOUR DIMENSIONS OF RESILIENCE

WHAT ARE THEY?

There are four dimensions that you can easily work with to develop your own resilience. Bear in mind that while these are separated conceptually, in practice they will overlap to some extent, and mutually reinforce each other.

These dimensions are:

 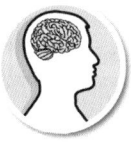  

Physical **Mental** **Emotional** **Social**

FOUR DIMENSIONS OF RESILIENCE

PHYSICAL

Every action you take is taken by your body, so it makes sense to keep your physical being in good shape (both literally and metaphorically).

If you look after your body, your body will look after you.

Here are some aspects that you can check, starting with:

Good nutrition. There's plenty of dietary advice out there for you. If it involves more fresh food and vegetables, less sugar and fewer calories, it's probably on the right track.

FOUR DIMENSIONS OF RESILIENCE

 **PHYSICAL**

Keep active. Exercise is important to keep your muscles toned. Whether you engage in regular sports or deliberately build it into your daily routines by walking from place to place and using stairs in preference to lifts and escalators, exercise counters all those hours spent sitting at a desk or looking at a screen.

Exercise for flexibility as much as for strength. Yoga and the Alexander Technique are both recommended for balance and flexibility.

Breathe. Check you are breathing fully, so that the oxygen gets plenty of chance to reach and restore your blood.

Sleep. You function better when you are well-rested. A short day-time nap can usefully supplement your night-time's sleep.

FOUR DIMENSIONS OF RESILIENCE

ENERGY GUZZLERS & SOURCES

You probably have a good sense of what saps your energy during the day. It might be working in a room with very little natural light or facing an especially miserable colleague.

By contrast perhaps you have noticed that opening a window or talking to a good friend boosts your energy levels.

Do you find it inspiring to display photos of your family or your friends on your desk?

Think about other pictures or objects you could keep around you to remind you of the good things in your life. Move them each week to refresh their impact.

FOUR DIMENSIONS OF RESILIENCE

ACTIVITY

Note down your top five energy guzzlers and your top five energy sources.

Choose one energy guzzler to tackle today – how can you avoid it or mitigate it, even a little?

And how can you draw inspiration from your energy sources and plan something energising today?

FOUR DIMENSIONS OF RESILIENCE

 ## MENTAL

Keeping your mind active and engaged supports your mental resilience.

Here's a quick mental arithmetic test for you:

> Start with 101, then subtract 7, and another 7, and so on until finally you reach a single digit figure: 101, 94, 87…

Whatever result you arrived at, the mental exercise was doing you good – though take care not to let any frustration at the task outweigh the positive effects on your brain circuitry.

More mental challenges to build into your routines:

- Quizzes
- Crosswords
- Jigsaws
- Sudoku
- Chess
- Card games
- Calming meditation
- Mindfulness
- Spiritual practice
- Detailed visualisations of positive future scenarios
- Mobile app games that stretch you or teach you something useful – map quizzes, for example

FOUR DIMENSIONS OF RESILIENCE

ACTIVITY – A LETTER FROM THE FUTURE

When you're oppressed by difficulties you are facing, pick a date in the future, say five years from now.

Now write a letter from your future self to your present self. Visualise a time when all your current woes have been solved and let your future self tell you about it. Explain how you found the solution and how much better life is now the problems have been solved.

The act of writing is a powerful tool for connecting with your own hidden resources. If you're able to visualise the desired outcome, it will be so much easier to turn it into a reality.

FOUR DIMENSIONS OF RESILIENCE

 **EMOTIONAL**

You will find emotional resilience in your nourishing store of feelings from times you have been happy, successful and resourceful.

When you remember those achievements you give yourself an emotional boost, along with useful reminders of how to do well.

The memory doesn't need to be anything grand or the sort of thing that would impress other people. It simply has to matter to you.

To find useful emotional memories, consider:

- Trips to interesting places
- Happy holidays
- Good relationships
- Successes in school
- Achievements in your hobbies
- Moments of good fortune
- Times you were proud of yourself
- Laughter with friends

FOUR DIMENSIONS OF RESILIENCE

 **ACTIVITY**

Find an object such as a favourite photo, a travel souvenir, a prize or a certificate, that reminds you of a time you flourished, when you felt good about yourself.

Recall the details of that time and remind yourself how well you felt and how skilfully you managed everything on that occasion.

Getting back in touch with those feelings from the past can help you do yourself justice again now.

You might like to make those items, or other tokens that prompt good feelings, more visible in your house or your office. Ambush yourself with emotional support!

FOUR DIMENSIONS OF RESILIENCE

 **SOCIAL**

Research from positive psychology tells us that a rich social life offers tremendous benefits, while isolation and loneliness can destroy your resilience.

If you have work colleagues, pick those with whom you would like to spend more time – perhaps using breaks to discover common interests beyond work.

If you enjoy their company, join in with social activities such as a drink or a meal out together. If none of that happens yet, you could be the one to start it.

Look beyond work and develop other sociable opportunities:
- A hobby you already enjoy…
- …Or start a new one
- Go out with friends
- Re-connect with old friends
- Join a network
- Or even spend more time with your family!

FOUR DIMENSIONS OF RESILIENCE

 COMMUNITIES OF SUPPORT

If you don't have a friend or colleague in your immediate environment, then look further afield. There may be support from a department at work – HR, perhaps, or a coaching facility. Or a professional body you subscribe to.

Because your struggles are not unique, there will be a community you can find on the internet. Every imaginable interest is catered for and there will be fellow sufferers (or enthusiasts) to call on who will understand what you are going through and know practical ways to do something about it.

You can start by simply reading what others are saying, which may be sufficient. Or you can take that extra sharing step of joining in with your own story.

FOUR DIMENSIONS OF RESILIENCE

ACTIVITY – SOCIAL STOCKTAKE

Make a chart of all your personal connections and see where there are opportunities to strengthen your links by meeting people more often, so that you get to do more of your favourite sociable activities.

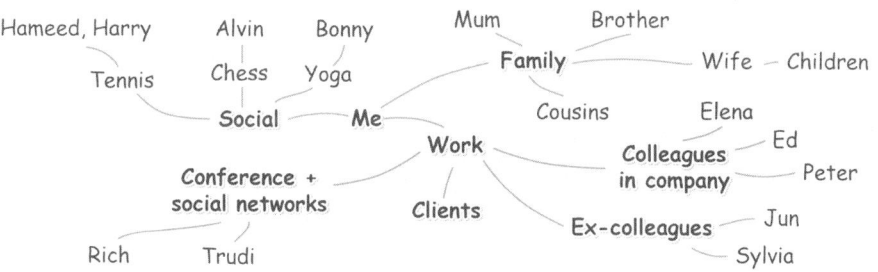

FOUR DIMENSIONS OF RESILIENCE

WHICH ROUTE TO TAKE?

All four of the dimensions of resilience will equip you to deal better with life's challenges. Sometimes it's a question of where to start.

If it is a problem to solve – the best thing to do is to start solving it.

If you cannot immediately tackle the problem, then take a moment to deal with the emotions involved, so that you are less stressed.

FOUR DIMENSIONS OF RESILIENCE

WHO YOU GONNA CALL?

Everyone at some point faces pain, fear or suffering. It is natural. And a trouble shared is, as they say, a trouble halved.

Who can you call when you need to talk something over, get help in a crisis? Is it reciprocal, and can they also call you?

Make sure that if you have a shoulder that friends or colleagues can cry on, they know about it.

And when you get into that kind of conversation, listen empathetically and listen with an ear for resourcefulness. Then the moments of darkness can lead to the greatest growth.

FOUR DIMENSIONS OF RESILIENCE

WORDS OF WISDOM

> 'You never know how strong you are until being strong is the only choice you have.'
> **Bob Marley**

> 'Only a man who knows what it is like to be defeated can reach down to the bottom of his soul and come up with the extra ounce of power it takes to win when the match is even.'
> **Muhammad Ali**

Resilience toolkit

RESILIENCE TOOLKIT

TOOLS THAT MAKE A DIFFERENCE

Building on the tips and techniques we've shared with you, this section of the book describes a set of resilience-building tools that you can apply daily. This toolkit will help you to:

- Keep perspective
- Focus on what you want to achieve
- Work with what you can influence rather than what you can't
- Identify what 'good' looks like, and rehearse how you will be when things are going well
- Appreciate your resources
- Focus on what's useful in any given situation
- Make progress towards your desired results with pragmatic and manageable small steps

RESILIENCE TOOLKIT

SOLUTIONS-FOCUSED TOOLS

The tools described on the following pages form the Solutions Focus toolkit, created by Paul Z Jackson and Mark McKergow for their book, *The Solutions Focus*, and based on the earlier work of Steve De Shazer and Insoo Kim Berg.

De Shazer and Berg set up the Brief Family Therapy Center (BFTC) in Milwaukee in the 1970s. They worked with the toughest of cases, including addiction, abuse and depression. The common factor was that their clients all needed to develop resilience first to cope with and then to overcome the life-threatening circumstances they found themselves in.

De Shazer and Berg discovered that patients made better progress when they were asked about what they wanted (solutions) instead of when they were asked about their problems.

RESILIENCE TOOLKIT

THE NATURE OF TOOLS

Before you start working, let's take a moment to unpack this metaphor and consider the nature of tools.

Depending on the job at hand, you pick up a particular tool and use it for a while. Then – equally importantly – you put it down, before selecting the appropriate tool for the next part of the job. To do this you need to know:

- What the tool does or might do
- How to use it – you'll have a degree of skill in the application
- When to pick it up
- When to put it down

If you are hanging a heavy picture on a hard wall, you'll need a drill and rawl plugs. In softer plaster, a hammer will do.

As you experience our toolkit, pictured on the next page, decide when it might be most useful for you to wield each tool.

RESILIENCE TOOLKIT

BUILDING A PLATFORM

Returning to the taxi analogy – you wouldn't tell the driver that you don't want to go to Marble Arch, as this gives no clue as to which direction you actually want to travel.

The same applies when you are building your platform. Many people focus on thinking and talking about what they don't want – and express this as the direction they don't wish to take.

You might say, for example, that you don't want to be so tired or stressed. Whilst it may well be true, it fails to identify what you **do** want, so we don't have a clear direction for travel.

RESILIENCE TOOLKIT

BUILDING A PLATFORM

When you find yourself stating what you don't want – ask yourself:

- *'What do I want instead?'*
- *'How will I know that I have what I want?'*
- *'What difference will this make for me?'*

Take the situation on the previous page. Rather than being stressed and tired, you might want to be able to find ways to relax more and be home by 5pm twice a week. Now you've constructed your platform. You have a clear enough idea of what's wanted, and you can start making progress towards it.

RESILIENCE TOOLKIT

FROM PROBLEM TO PLATFORM

Practise building your platforms. Jot down your problem, using a grid similar to the one here, then ask yourself what you want instead, and list the benefits.
Then you'll know more clearly if it's really
something worth working on.

Problems/ Issues	What do you want? Goals	Benefits

RESILIENCE TOOLKIT

FUTURE PERFECT

> Suppose that overnight, while you are asleep, your problems vanish and things are now as you would like them to be. When you wake up, how will you know?

Knowing what you want is a great start to building resilience. You can make this even more impactful and helpful by using your imagination to conjure up detailed visions of what you want. Positive mental attitude turned out to be the main requirement for survivors in the toughest of situations, says Laurence Gonzales in his book, *Deep Survival: Who Lives, Who Dies and Why*.

This description of how you would like things to be, dubbed the **future perfect**, gives you a vision to aspire to and a set of reference points for recognising aspects that are working out as you wish.

RESILIENCE TOOLKIT

YOUR FUTURE PERFECT

First, write down what you want (your platform).

Now ask yourself the following questions to articulate your future perfect:

> Suppose, overnight while you are asleep, your problems vanish, and things are now as you would like them to be...

- When you wake up, how will you know?
- What's the first thing you notice that tells you things are better?
- What are you doing?
- What do other people notice about you?
- How are they responding to you?
- What else do you notice or do this day that tells you that you are on track?

The more detail you can capture, the better.

RESILIENCE TOOLKIT

SCALE
MEASURING PROGRESS

We're all familiar with the idea of measuring on a scale of 1-10. Unfortunately, scales are sometimes used to identify gaps or beat ourselves and others up for not achieving top marks. Here's a way of using **scales** as a tool to build resources, identify what's working and make progress.

On a scale of 1-10, where 10 represents what you want and 1 is the opposite (no part of what you want ever happens) – where would you place yourself? Let's call that 'n'.

Simply by placing yourself on a scale, you have implicitly accepted the possibility of progress and movement. If you can be at 3, then it's possible to imagine being at 4 or 5. You're first going to focus on what's got you as high as 'n', rather than wondering why you are not at 10. It's appreciating the distance travelled that will bolster your resilience, rather than fretting about reasons for failure or obstacles ahead.

Now, wherever you've placed yourself on the scale, ask yourself – what have I done to reach that far? What resources and skills did I use? What would other people say has got me this high?

RESILIENCE TOOLKIT

SCALE
WHEN THINGS ARE REALLY TOUGH

You can also use a scale to give yourself a perspective on the events troubling you, ranging from 1 for disappointment to 10 for disaster.

On a scale of 1 to 10, where 10 is the worst it could be and 1 is neutral, where are you now?

If you are not at 10, things could clearly be worse than they are, so you already have some progress in the bag.

By working with a scale, you are accepting the possibility of things being better (elsewhere on the scale). You have the key resilience ingredients of **hope** and **possibility**.

RESILIENCE TOOLKIT

COUNTERS

WHAT COUNTS, WHAT'S USEFUL

The idea of **counters** is to make a collection of anything that might count as one of your resilience resources. This can include times from the past when you feel you have been particularly resilient, a list of your skills and your character strong points, a map of your strongest social relationships… anything that serves as evidence of personal resilience.

You have already practised identifying counters when using a scale, by asking yourself how you are that high on the scale. The evidence you produce to justify the figure you award yourself is testimony to your resilience. Also ask, *'What's the highest you've been on the scale?'* The best it's been in the past can offer you a reassuring, confidence-building story of how you can be resilient again now or the next time you need to be.

RESILIENCE TOOLKIT

YOUR COUNTERS

Think of a situation that's troubling you at the moment.

Ask yourself, *'On a scale of 1-10 where 1 is* 'I have no resources to deal with this' *and 10 is* 'I am fully equipped to handle this situation', *where are you now?'*

Write down a list of all the resources, skills and experiences that have got you this high on the scale. List anything else that 'counts' that will be useful for you in this endeavour.

These are your **counters**, ready as a resilience bank account to draw on when needed.

RESILIENCE TOOLKIT

AFFIRM

WHAT ARE YOU IMPRESSED WITH?

We can all be highly self-critical at times and forget to acknowledge our good points. This is modesty to a fault: the fault being that it detracts from our resilience.

Instead of listing your faults and dwelling on your failings and shortcomings, try articulating your strengths, your better traits and your positive characteristics. If it's really too difficult for you to do this for yourself, enlist the help of a friend or a professional coach.

Writing these qualities down or stating them out loud gives them greater resonance. Once they are, so to speak, on the table, it's easier to bring them into play in your current interactions and get them working well for you. So make manifest anything that is working and useful.

RESILIENCE TOOLKIT

AFFIRM

REFLECTING ON THE DAY

You don't need to wait until you do something spectacularly impressive to give yourself a pat on the back. Simply reflecting on your day in a resourceful way can put this tool to good use on your path to sustainable resilience.

Find a suitable opportunity at the end of the day for a moment of reflection and ask yourself the following:

- What went well today?
- Pick three things you are pleased with: what pleased you about each of them?
- What do they tell you about your good qualities and practices?
- How might these qualities and practices be useful to you tomorrow?
- What else went well today?

RESILIENCE TOOLKIT

SMALL ACTIONS
MAKING PROGRESS

The best way to get unstuck is to do something. Almost anything will do. Movement prevents hopelessness. Changing one thing may alter all sorts of other things. Give it a go and become an agent, the principal actor in your own drama.

A single small step has several advantages over a big step or many small steps. It is less daunting and so you are more likely to do it. A discrete small step allows you to pause for reflection. Did it help? If so, do some more or continue in the same direction. If not, then little has been lost, and you can reconsider, recalibrate and take a different small step.

A small step has the feel of experimentation: you are doing something to see what happens. A small step will attract less attention than a big step, so you will feel less pressure from observers.

RESILIENCE TOOLKIT

YOUR SMALL ACTIONS

Think about something that's been bothering you recently.

What's the **smallest action** you can take that will help you get unstuck? Write it down.

Remember, make it really small. This might be something like jotting down a note, packing an item in your bag for tomorrow or even as simple as smiling at a couple of people.

A colleague of ours who was having difficulties at work decided to smile at more people on the train during her daily commute. Within a few weeks she made a number of 'commuter buddies'. She reported that seeing friendly faces and chatting on the train had made a significant difference to how she felt when she got to work, and in turn how she dealt with the daily office challenges.

RESILIENCE TOOLKIT

WHAT ELSE?

Rather than stopping once you've uncovered a few counters, given yourself a meaningful affirmation or advanced a suitable small step, take a moment to check in and ask yourself **what else?**

A review gives you the chance to find anything useful that you might have missed. There is usually something. The task is to find it.

Next time you are using any of the tools, or reflecting on something that's worked, ask yourself, *'What else might be useful to note here?'*

You can:

- **Deepen** the pool of resources, by diving into more detail about the aspects you are finding helpful
- **Widen** the range of resources, by finding tangential information and ideas from further afield

RESILIENCE TOOLKIT

THE POWER OF REVIEW

In our fast-moving world, it's tempting to shift relentlessly from one activity to another without taking time to stop, reflect and take note of what's different or what's better, even a little bit. Your final tool, **what's better?**, is for picking up when you can afford a few moments of reflection.

You'll have noticed there's a theme with these solutions-focused tools – they are all pointing you in the direction of what is working, rather than what isn't; what you can do, rather than what you can't.

'What's better?' is no exception. In those moments of reflection, ask yourself *'What's got better since I last looked?'* Identify recent progress, wherever it came from. This will give you useful topical information and clues about what's currently useful and what you might do next.

Whatever has been helpful lately in this particular context may well indicate your best next steps. At the very least, it will highlight more possibilities.

RESILIENCE TOOLKIT

A FINAL THOUGHT

> 'A positive mind is the sharpest tool that brings down the monuments of failure. The quickest way to fail is to murder your mind with negative thoughts!'
> **Israelmore Ayivor**, Daily Drive 365

Mistakes & Progress, Failure & Recovery

MISTAKES & PROGRESS, FAILURE & RECOVERY

JOIN THE ANTI-PERFECTIONIST LEAGUE

Sometimes in life and in work we demand perfection. If you were piloting a passenger aircraft, running a nuclear power plant or operating on my kidney, perfection would be welcome. Mistakes here have big bad consequences.

Elsewhere it is fine for your performance to be acceptable rather than perfect. In such circumstances, you are not crushed by your mistakes and can stop beating yourself up. Focusing on mistakes is likely to generate unhelpful emotions, such as fear.

Focusing on getting it right, with a useful state of mind, such as calm, confident concentration, gets better results. To remain resilient, it's important to keep trying new activities and learning new skills. If you make mistakes along the way, that's fine – how you deal with them is all part of the learning and an important component of keeping your resilience muscles in good shape.

MISTAKES & PROGRESS, FAILURE & RECOVERY

ARE YOU PERFECT?

Are you perfect? Have you gone through life without ever making any mistakes? If you can answer 'Yes', then you are in for a resilience-shattering shock when you do eventually stumble.

The best bet is to let go of unnecessary tendencies towards perfectionism. Perfectionism is exhausting. Take up an attitude of experimentation and having a go, then learn from the variety of results. That's what develops your resilience, building your skills for bouncing back from mistakes, failures and disappointments.

The learning is in the bounceback — the eventual success made all the more satisfying by the backdrop of the negative.

Our difficulties bring into relief our resources of stoicism, endurance and plain coping. It's sweet to be reminded of these, even when the only learning from the mistake is 'don't do that again' – which oftentimes we already knew.

MISTAKES & PROGRESS, FAILURE & RECOVERY

ON A SCALE OF 1 TO 10...

Demanding perfection is unrealistic. Instead, aim to create a sense of what's good enough (or what's better). Then think about what progress you can make towards whatever you are trying to achieve.

Express this on a scale: if 1 is absolutely unacceptable and 10 is absolute perfection, how high is good enough? Let's say it's 7: make sure you are clear what 7 represents for you and what it would look like to anyone else involved.

If you are currently at 6, you can see exactly where you are doing well and the difference needed to reach the expected standard – leaving you well placed to take appropriate measures to improve the quality.

This is not about low standards. It is about standards that are appropriate for the task in hand.

MISTAKES & PROGRESS, FAILURE & RECOVERY

THE TRAPS OF PERFECTIONISM

One trap of perfectionism is that if you suspect you may be less than perfect, you may never get started at all. It's too risky. So perfectionism inhibits your creativity. And you need to be constantly on the learning edge to avoid stagnation and to keep developing your resilience in a changing world.

Another trap is that the perfectionist is reluctant to admit to a mistake and so mistakes go unacknowledged – or worse, are covered up.

When you reduce any unnecessary fear of making mistakes, you function more smoothly and make fewer mistakes. So how can you reduce fear even in circumstances where mistakes matter and are rightly discouraged?

If you are less harsh on yourself when making a mistake, you will recover more quickly and deploy more energy into returning to the activity in a better state. That's resilience in action.

MISTAKES & PROGRESS, FAILURE & RECOVERY

MIND YOUR LANGUAGE

The language you use has a direct impact on how you view failures and mistakes, which in turn influences what you do next. The temptation is to focus on what didn't work, why you got it wrong and who's to blame.

Instead, you can review events in a more useful and effective way.

Rather than focusing on deficits, failure, what hasn't worked, blame and difficulty, you can re-phrase your questions and statements to draw attention to ability, resources, contribution and knowledge. Make sure to stay aware of what **has** been achieved, especially when it's so tempting to recall only what hasn't.

Before you begin a challenging task, assume that there is a way to succeed and allow your mind to explore those possibilities.

Think of a time where you messed up, where something didn't go as planned, where you made a mistake. Now ask yourself both sets of questions on the next page and notice the difference.

MISTAKES & PROGRESS, FAILURE & RECOVERY

RECOVERING FROM FAILURE

Direct Route
- What were you aiming to achieve?
- What went well, even a little bit?
- Which aspects did you personally handle well, even to some extent?
- Which of your skills and resources did you use in this situation?
- How might you influence others to contribute to moving this forward?
- What will be the first small signs that you are making progress?
- What advice would you give yourself for next time?

Potential Excursions
- What went wrong?
- What were the consequences?
- How did you contribute to the poor outcome?
- What didn't you do?
- Who or what caused the difficulty?
- What barriers do you face?
- Why will it be difficult to take this forward now?

MISTAKES & PROGRESS, FAILURE & RECOVERY

AFTER A CRISIS, ASK WHAT WORKED

When something goes wrong, the temptation is immediately to start analysing everything and assigning blame.

But you can increase resilience by looking at how you got through it and what actually worked, as this holds the key to improving morale and doing better next time by not repeating mistakes.

MISTAKES & PROGRESS, FAILURE & RECOVERY

FIGHT, FLIGHT, FREEZE OR FLOW

When you face a new challenge, you have two visceral responses: fight or flight. These are instinctive, the product of evolution, allowing survival instincts to cut in, with flight representing a swift escape from the sabre-tooth tiger. You know you have little chance of winning, so you run away. Or if you are suddenly attacked, you may instinctively fight. It's automatic.

The diagram illustrates the tensions between the typical responses to a potentially stresful moment.

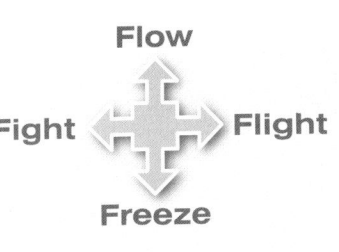

MISTAKES & PROGRESS, FAILURE & RECOVERY

FIGHT, FLIGHT, FREEZE OR FLOW

While there are few sabre-tooth tigers around these days, the behaviour is hardwired by evolution and kicks in as a response even to lesser threats. It takes the system a while to recover from these adrenaline shots, which is why much modern life, with constant stimulus and insufficient opportunity to do all that's needed physically to regain equilibrium, can be so damagingly stressful.

With **freeze**, you are rooted to the spot. In many cases this is a poor strategy unless you become invisible. Deer and other animals do successfully use stillness or camouflage to hide, or rely on their lack of aggression to neutralise attacking intent.

In martial arts such as aikido you fight by means of **flow**, combining your opponent's energy with your own, a very neat improvisational use of immediate resources.

Flow is the improvisational response, available to you when you are at your most resilient. Face the circumstance and adapt to it in the moment as it emerges and evolves.

MISTAKES & PROGRESS, FAILURE & RECOVERY

GO WITH THE FLOW

If you can get into a state of flow, or what athletes call 'in the zone', you'll make fewer mistakes, enjoy yourself more, and prove more resilient.

Psychologist Mihály Csikszentmihályi researched and popularised the concept of *'Flow'*.

Take a look at this diagram:

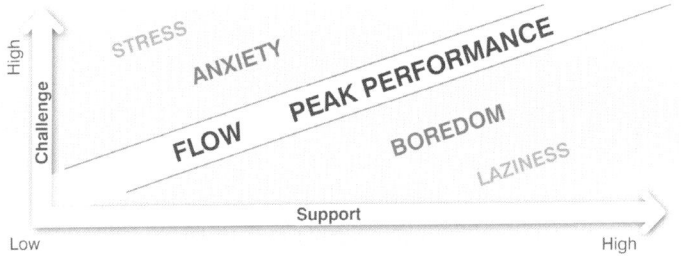

On the x axis, there's the degree of support available to you, rising from low to high. The y axis represents the rising degree of the challenge that you face.

MISTAKES & PROGRESS, FAILURE & RECOVERY

GO WITH THE FLOW

Where your support and your challenge are more or less matched, you are in your channel of flow. There we relish excitement, adventure and stretch; and in an organisational setting, we expect innovation and achievement.

If the degree of support is high, but the challenge is too easy – let's say you've been doing the same routine job for many years – you may grow bored and disengaged.

Conversely, if you're being pushed to exceed all previous targets, while under-resourced and poorly supported or lacking the necessary skills, then you are likely to fail. You also have a recipe for anxiety and stress. High stress can damage your health and chip away at your resilience reserves.

Flow feels good and produces physical and chemical effects on the body with endorphins and energy. Your activity seems effortless, easy and elegant.

MISTAKES & PROGRESS, FAILURE & RECOVERY

HOW TO USE THE FLOW MODEL

The model (see page 91) indicates what to do if you want to increase your prospects of flow. You either increase or reduce the level of challenge, or increase or reduce the level of support.

Suppose at work you are stressed by a situation or by too much exposure to a particular individual, then a good strategy is to seek more support from colleagues. The key is to recognise what is going on and then take action to get to a better place of flow.

Experiences of flow increase our resilience, while stress and boredom diminish those resources.

It's relatively easy to combat stress by learning new skills or seeking more support; get training or schedule a rest. It's also often possible to alter the level of challenge; by negotiating the tasks you are set or lowering the level of ambition.

MISTAKES & PROGRESS, FAILURE & RECOVERY

HOW TO USE THE FLOW MODEL

Equally, if you are a manager, then you are in a good position to notice how your reports are faring. You can adjust their schedules or allocate training or support to reduce the work load, a quick remedy to avoid longer-lasting burnout, absenteeism, resentment and need for replacements.

Or, if a colleague is under-stretched, consider increasing the challenge, by delegating a new project, offering more responsibility or reducing the amount of assistance.

The model might also persuade you to reduce damaging self-judgement. Rather than imagining yourself to be poor at a task, or accepting boredom as your natural lot, you can recognise your position on the graph and make the necessary adjustments.

> 'Of all the virtues we can learn, no trait is more useful, more essential for survival, and more likely to improve the quality of life than the ability to transform adversity into an enjoyable challenge.'
> **Mihály Csikszentmihályi**

MISTAKES & PROGRESS, FAILURE & RECOVERY

APPLYING THE MODEL TO YOUR OWN WORK

Notice where certain activities take you.

- If you find yourself stressed, take a note of what seems to be causing it, and see if you can change one or more of those elements. Then note the difference.
- If you are bored, what does it take to get you animated again?
- If you are in flow, what happened to get you there?
  Can you put those conditions into play again?
- What challenge can you add to increase your feelings of enjoyably developing your talents or stretching your abilities?
- What extra support can you put into place to guard against overload or burnout?

Take time to jot down some thoughts.

MISTAKES & PROGRESS, FAILURE & RECOVERY

SOLUTIONS NOT PROBLEMS

It's good practice to focus on what you want, if only on the basis that this is motivational, compared to the negativity of looking at what you don't want. Knowing what you don't want is OK, but tells you surprisingly little most of the time about what you do want. The 'opposite' is not always obvious.

Knowing what you want immediately prompts ideas about what actions you might take, and guides you towards indicators of the progress you're making.

Recently Janine couldn't find her slippers. *'It was a cold day and I have wooden floors in my house. The temptation was to berate myself for losing yet another thing, wonder why I was so disorganised and then spend hours looking for my slippers. Instead I realised that what I wanted was warm feet, and simply put on a pair of thick socks. The slippers turned up eventually.'*

The problem and solution are not always related.

MISTAKES & PROGRESS, FAILURE & RECOVERY

THE PROGRESS PRINCIPLE

It's worth being aware of the importance of progress. As pioneering Austrian endocrinologist Hans Selye says, a stressor is essentially neutral. Our experience of eustress (that's stress that is good) or distress is a result of whether we believe we are winning or losing. This links extremely well with the Progress Principle, developed recently by Harvard Business School Professor Teresa Amabile and psychologist Steven Kramer.

Amabile and Kramer discovered that top performers need to experience 'forward momentum in meaningful work,' and they suggest managers should manage for progress. And psychologist Edward John Boyd Barrett suggested that our motivation for doing anything was to *'Survive, survive on one's own terms, or improve one's capacity for independent action.'*

All three bodies of research demonstrate the importance of the story you tell yourself about what you are doing, why you are doing it and your interpretation of the results.

MISTAKES & PROGRESS, FAILURE & RECOVERY

THE PROGRESS PRINCIPLE

These are all factors to consider as you look to get more positive stress and less negative. For example, tackling what you perceive to be unnecessary red tape will cost you much more than responding to a demanding client request you deem justified.

The answer to dissolving sustained workplace stress is not deep breathing or meditation: it's a focus on mastery through engagement, focus, and capacity building. Find a meaningful goal you can't achieve and figure out how to achieve it.

> 'I have not failed, I've just found 10,000 ways that won't work.'
> **Thomas A Edison**

> 'Failure is temporary but giving up is permanent.'
> **Kiran Mazumdar-Shaw**, MD of India's largest biotech company, Biocon

TEAMS: SPREADING RESILIENCE

TEAMS: SPREADING RESILIENCE

THE IMPACT

So far we've focused predominantly on individual resilience, yet what about the teams you belong to or influence?

Experts tell us there are many factors required for a team to be effective, including a shared purpose or goal, clearly defined tasks, diverse and relevant skill sets, and clear lines of communication.

The ability to leverage these factors often depends on the team's resilience, its ability to absorb change, adapt and respond to challenging events in a resourceful and coherent way.

What difference would it make if your team could be more resilient?

What's required, and what can you do?

TEAMS: SPREADING RESILIENCE

FLOURISHING IN ADVERSITY

When, in 2010, 33 Chilean miners were trapped 700 metres below ground after a cave-in, they kept themselves active physically and spiritually. First, they tried to escape. Not possible! Then they shared leadership duties with democratic voting and rationed food; and above all they maintained a sense of reality and acceptance, and focused on survival.

You and the teams you are part of can help yourselves to be tenacious and persevering by keeping a sense of humour, defining yourselves as always up for a challenge and being aware of the importance of bouncing back from defeats or loss. Within the team, you can demonstrate and encourage sharing stories of success.

You can set yourselves up for more success by managing the expectations of team members, seeking and developing personal and team strategies to change a losing streak.

TEAMS: SPREADING RESILIENCE

IMPROVING THE ATMOSPHERE

Firstly you need to create an environment that is conducive to bouncing back.

This can be done by improving the atmosphere to one of a collaborative culture, so that the team is not shaken to the foundations by every little setback, knock or challenge.

A more positive environment means that any member of the team can signal that you are all ready to rise to the occasion.

The whole is greater than the sum of its parts, but only if the parts are well connected and well disposed towards each other. That means communication is working effectively, and there is a sense of being a collective, with shared purpose and a readiness to find the resources within the team and allocate them promptly to deal with the needs of the situation.

Some ways to do this make up the rest of this chapter.

TEAMS: SPREADING RESILIENCE

WHAT'S GOING WELL – TEAM MEETINGS

Whenever you have team meetings, start by talking about what's going right rather than any problems that have arisen. Have a quick round-the-table discussion, where everyone spends 30 seconds sharing one item that has gone well for them since the last meeting. This sets the tone for your gathering, making it more enjoyable and productive, even if there are problems to be discussed.

If you do this regularly, people will start noticing what's going well because they know they're going to be asked about it. They'll be scanning their memories for this material even as they are travelling to the meeting. And that builds resilience, because they're focusing on their successes rather than their failures, raising the energy in times when it might be low.

TEAMS: SPREADING RESILIENCE

TELL EMPOWERING STORIES

Stories are powerful. Take advantage of this when developing resilient teams and use stories to communicate rather than commands.

Sometimes if you tell people what to do, it can undermine their confidence, as they feel like the manager is controlling them rather than leaving them choices. Tell them stories of achievement instead of just issuing instructions, and allow them to extract the advice they need rather than imposing it on them.

For example, if someone is regularly late for work, avoid saying, *'Show up on time!'* Tell them, *'I was just speaking to Hanna and she says she has made her journey a lot quicker by taking a different route on the underground. She hasn't been late since.'*

TEAMS: SPREADING RESILIENCE

DISPLAY SUCCESS

Remember how good it feels when somebody notices something you've done well, and comments on this in an authentic way. Imagine if this was on show for others to see.

A simple and effective way of building team resourcefulness and spreading the energy and positivity that this engenders is to create a success board. This is a place where team members can post notes, capturing what others have done that they are impressed and pleased with.

A team in Reading Borough Council tried this out. They told us that people were a bit reluctant at first, yet as notes started to appear, those receiving compliments were so touched and pleased that they also started to write notes for others. Before long the board was a permanent fixture in the staff room.

TEAMS: SPREADING RESILIENCE

FIND OUT WHAT'S WANTED

If your team is discussing an issue and you notice energy draining, with people getting demotivated, it may be because you've got stuck in the problem or what's not working. Instead of talking about the problem and what has caused it, ask the group what they want instead. Shift the focus from the problem to the desired outcome. For example, instead of discussing what was to blame for missing sales targets, ask what ideas people have for increasing sales.

This is a far more resourceful approach, as it's perfectly possible that the cause of the problem is out of your control. If so, there is no value in focusing on it, but discussing the desired outcome may reveal a new solution that you'd never have considered otherwise.

TEAMS: SPREADING RESILIENCE

MORE SOCIABILITY AT WORK

You build resilience by having a good time, especially when you are having your fun socially, with other people. The experience of connection builds collective resilience, which supports each of us as individuals.

At work, set up events so that people will look forward to a good time, join in and then talk about it. Supporting each other builds resilience for you all.

Encourage social networks and peer coaching groups to prevent isolation and maintain cohesion and support. Giving help goes well with asking for help: people appreciate mutuality and shared experiences.

TEAMS: SPREADING RESILIENCE

FINDING FAULT OR FUTURE FOCUS?

When something goes disastrously wrong, the temptation is to start analysing everything immediately and assigning blame. But it's more useful to look at how you got through it and what worked, as this holds the key to improved performance next time.

An Austrian electricity supply company had sent a letter to all their customers informing them of inaccurate price rises. The switchboard had been jammed with complaints, with customers threatening to leave.

Manager Hans, who led the ensuing senior team review, bravely began by writing 'What went well?' onto the flipchart and opened a discussion on the positive aspects of the incident – how quickly they had sent out a corrective letter, the courtesy and speed with which everyone, including senior managers, had dealt with the phone calls, the teamwork shown in co-ordinating their response. The meeting ended with exploration of ways to prevent the problem recurring. There was no need to discuss what had gone wrong.

Allocating blame demotivates people and rarely fixes the problem. By looking at how they resolved the problem, both team and organisation became more resilient.

TEAMS: SPREADING RESILIENCE

QUOTES & ACTION

Task: Think about the members of a work team you belong to – what have they done recently that you have been impressed with? How might you share this with them?

> 'I am fundamentally an optimist. Whether that comes from nature or nurture, I cannot say. Part of being an optimist is keeping one's head pointed toward the sun, one's feet moving forward.'
> **Nelson Mandela**

> 'When you start out in a team, you have to get the teamwork going and then you get something back.'
> **Michael Schumacher**

TEAMS: SPREADING RESILIENCE

IN CONCLUSION

Now it's up to you.

You can influence what happens.

Your resilience is simply a matter of connecting to your resources so that you respond well to whatever the world brings your way.

> *'Don't give up, normally it is the last key on the ring which opens the door.'*
> **Paulo Coelho**

FURTHER INFORMATION

SUGGESTED READING

Macmillan Dictionary
http://www.macmillandictionary.com/buzzword/entries/bouncebackability

The Solutions Focus - Making Coaching and Change SIMPLE, Paul Z Jackson & Mark McKergow. Nicholas Brealey, 2006

Positively Speaking – The Art of Constructive Conversations with a Solutions Focus, Paul Z Jackson & Janine Waldman. The Solutions Focus, 2010

The 7 Habits of Highly Effective People, Stephen Covey. Simon and Schuster, 2004

Tough at the Top? New Rules of Resilience for Women's Leadership Success, Sarah Bond & Gillian Shapiro, 2014

Deep Survival: Who Lives, Who Dies and Why, Laurence Gonzales. W. W. Norton & Company, 2005

The Progress Principle: Using Small Wins to Ignite Joy, Engagement and Creativity at Work, Teresa Amabile & Steven Kramer. Harvard Business School, 2011

Motive-Force and Motivation-Tracks, a Research in Will Psychology, Edward John Boyd Barrett. Longmans, Green & Co., reissued in 2016

Hans Selye: http://www.stress.org/about/hans-selye-birth-of-stress/

About the Authors

Janine Waldman and **Paul Z Jackson** are leaders in the application of Solutions Focus in the UK and around the world. As co-directors of TSF, they provide coaching, training and consultancy to clients including Care UK, Tate, Nivea and Reading Borough Council. Find more at www.thesolutionsfocus.co.uk.

Janine Waldman MSc FCIPD specialises in coaching and training. She has over 20 years' experience in consultancy and organisational development, having previously held senior HRD positions in the UK and New Zealand. A fellow of the CIPD, she is a visiting lecturer on HRD and leadership programmes, and has taught on post-graduate programmes at Birkbeck College and University of Westminster.

Paul Z Jackson MA (Oxon) is an inspirational consultant, who applies his expertise in improvisation, accelerated learning and the solutions focus approach to programmes in strategy, leadership, teamwork, creativity and innovation. He draws on his experiences in journalism, comedy production and at the BBC to create impactful workshops that connect directly to the needs of the participants.